The Book of
Sensual
Massage

The Book of
Sensual
Massage

Christine Unseld-Baumanns

Sterling Publishing Co., Inc.   New York

Cover photo and
photography: Foto Design
Hesselmann (BFF), München

Translated by Elisabeth E. Reinersmann
Edited by Laurel Ornitz

10 9 8 7 6 5 4 3 2 1

English translation © 1990 by Sterling Publishing Company
387 Park Avenue South, New York, N.Y. 10016
Original edition published under the title
Partnermassage: Streicheleinheiten für Körper und Seele
© 1989 by Falken-Verlag GmbH, 6272 Niedernhausen/Ts., West Germany
Distributed in Canada by Sterling Publishing
% Canadian Manda Group, P.O. Box 920, Station U
Toronto, Ontario, Canada M8Z 5P9
Distributed in Great Britain and Europe by Cassell PLC
Villiers House, 41/47 Strand, London WC2N 5JE
Distributed in Australia by Capricorn Ltd.
P.O. Box 665, Lane Cove, NSW 2066
Printed in Hong Kong
All rights reserved

ISBN 0-8069-7379-X

Contents

Tuning In to Sensuousness

The Journey Across the Body

The longing for touch seems to be innate; it is a yearning we have from the first day of our life. As we experience touch, caresses, and being held, the need for touch seems to increase more and more. In other words, we develop an appetite for it—at first through our mother's gentle caresses; then through the discovery of our own body, and the tender, exploring touches of our first boyfriend or girlfriend; and later through the embrace of a lover, when everything inside of us seems to resonate with sheer pleasure.

Touch, as a stimulant and a form of human interaction, has a language all its own. A touch is often able to communicate something that is difficult to put into words. A touch can say: "I like you, you are wonderful, I need you," or: "I want you to be comfortable with me."

A massage is one of the most wonderful gifts that two people in love can give to each other. A massage can provide more than mere enjoyment; it is a way that you and your partner can experience mutual trust—without reservation, without limits. This trust is essential in order to fully receive and give real pleasure. To be able to surrender yourself to a massage from your partner says to your partner: "I am willing to let go, to become vulnerable, to allow closeness, and to be open to intimacy."

But even though we long for closeness and intimacy and to be touched, partners in relationships often short-change each other by neglecting this "journey across the body." In spite of the sexual revolution, many people deprive themselves of pleasure as a result of the taboos that still exist that hinder uninhibited touching and sensuality.

Being uninhibited means to be able to give and receive sensual joy freely and unconditionally, without asking where will it lead—or, moreover, expecting that it *must* lead to intercourse. Such sexual expectations can create performance pressure in men. Sexual expectations may result from a faulty understanding of emancipation in which women assume that intercourse is a right to be collected. This pressure surely undermines any ability to freely enjoy the pleasure of a sensual massage. Sexual expectations are a dilemma for women as well. Depending on her physical state or psychological mood, a woman might want a sensual massage—just that and nothing more. Partner massage is not synonymous with sex, and it's a mistaken assumption to think that it must lead to orgasm.

But remember, partner massage has no written rules; whatever happens is entirely determined by the two people involved. The gift of a massage might, of course, have as its highest point the sexual act. After all, it might awaken sexual desire of such intensity that nothing else would do. But it's also possible that, say, after a long hard day of work, a massage will create such deep relaxation that every trace of stress and tension is wiped away. At these times, you may feel as though your soul has wings and nothing beyond the massage is needed.

Another fallacy: Receiving a massage is the same as becoming helpless, being at the mercy of the hands of the other person. This fear seems to be rooted deep in our subconscious mind and is not totally unfounded. Those who have experienced the joy of partner massage have no doubt felt with some surprise and maybe a certain amount of fear the awesome energies and strong emotions that seem to flow like magnetic waves between the two partners. Men, especially, are often surprised to find themselves with such strong reactions to the touch of bodily zones that they either did not know were pleasure points or had deliberately ignored. They often feel overwhelmed by the intensity of their emotions yet pleased when they begin to experience an ever increasing ability to let go of old control mechanisms and surrender to their partner.

Every partner massage can be a totally new sensual experience. Our skin, the body's largest organ, is our connection to the outside world. It has thousands of minute nerve endings that are in direct contact with the pleasure center in the brain. Every touch, therefore, can elicit strong sensations that are received by our brain, and are messages that we intensely long for. They tell us: "I love to touch you because I like you. You are not alone."

Sensitively touching a partner with your hands, hair, or lips can transmit warmth and create trust in a new relationship. It can also revitalize a stale relationship that is stuck in routine. This is because partner massage stimulates the joyful expectation for interpersonal communication in the widest sense of its meaning. What makes all of this so much fun is that partners who long for tenderness can have it without any sexual expectations or pressures.

And don't you believe that only professional massage therapists can be good at it. If you use your own sensitivity and intuitive ability, you will be able to discover the mood and physical condition of your partner and you will know what will make him/her feel good. For instance, after a day full of stress and tension, you will know if there is a need for a rigorous, deep massage, or if the skin is so delicate and sensitive that only a tender stroking of the muscles is called for. "Listen" with your hands. "Listen" with your entire body to find out what your partner wants and needs most. This way, you can do no wrong. It will be like a dance where you allow yourself to fall into the rhythm of your partner. The motions are loose, relaxed. The flow is easy, not tense; nothing is forced. The more two people allow themselves the pleasure of a partner massage, the more they will be able to luxuriate in the pleasure. Trust your body and the messages it gives you; say yes to them, accept them. Only then can you give pleasure and enjoy the adventure called "partner massage."

Before you begin, make sure that nothing will disturb you. Disconnect the phone and the doorbell, and think only of yourself and your partner.

Before the Massage

Taking a bath together is an ideal beginning for a partner massage. The soothing warmth of the water will not only relieve tension and tightness, but it will also create an atmosphere of trust, allowing you and your partner to let go. You will both enjoy being soaped, and having a clean body will add to your feeling of self-confidence. But a joint bath also sets the stage for the process of stroking and touching that is to come. You will know that you can trust the hands that will be touching you later. And if you finish with a hand shower, it will rinse off any soap and take away any residue of awkwardness. A well-cared-for body is a beautiful body, and feeling good about your body will add to the sense of well-being and contentment that you will experience in a partner massage.

To make sure that your massage will be a total success, have all the necessary accouterments on hand: an aromatic massage oil (possibly on a little plate warmer to make it pleasant to the skin) or a body cream that will glide easily over the skin, pretty towels, maybe a long, soft feather, incense or an aromatic candle, and—unless you both prefer total silence—soft music. Know what your partner's preferences are and use your imagination. It's a good idea to check with your partner as to which massage oil he/she would like on a given day because the aroma of an essential oil contributes greatly to the overall effect of a massage. Certain essential oils will help to stimulate vital energies, whereas others will help to release tension. Partner massage is in part aroma therapy, a form of therapy that makes use of the properties of essential oils in order to support psychological harmony and alleviate physical tension. These oils increase the effectiveness of a massage because they penetrate the skin and the aroma gently soothes the senses.

A massage oil containing orange blossom, lavender, or balm oil is perfect for releasing tension, and one with rosemary or lemon oil is great for awakening the senses. But you might want to surprise your partner by creating your own massage oil. Mix your partner's favorite perfume or cologne into a neutral base oil, like almond oil. You can't go wrong.

The room temperature is very important. Make sure that you both are warm; nothing will spoil a well-intentioned loving massage faster than chills.

The massage itself can be done on a sofa, bed, or massage table, and many people prefer to do it on the floor. Let your partner stretch out on your favorite colorful, thick bath towel. You will be able to reach him/her from all sides without having to strain yourself. And you'll be able to easily perform all phases of the massage, like applying pressure or kneading, pushing, or stroking, whether you are kneeling, sitting, or sitting on your haunches.

Choosing the proper lighting is also important. The softer the light, the easier it will be for both of you to take in every touch with every pore of your skin and to concentrate on each other.

To add to the ambiance, choose music that your partner is particularly fond of, but just make sure that it plays softly in the background. The two of you should fill the room, not the music. At this moment, there is nothing more important in this world than your partner and yourself and your shared joy and comfort. Remember, everything is allowed that brings joy to your partner and yourself. Discover together your very own rituals that give the greatest pleasure.

In addition to the sensitive touch of your hands, bring your hair and your lips—all of your creativity and imagination—to this massage. Use color, incense, music, so that all of your senses come into play.

The Language of Touch

Are you aware of all the power and sensitivity that reside in your hands? In a partner massage, let yourself discover—rediscover—the joy of physical touch that you probably knew as a child without inhibition. Give the occasion of a partner massage a special meaning; make it a "holiday" for two. It will bring you emotionally and physically closer. At the outset, agree with your partner as to who at that particular time will be the giver and who will be the receiver.

If you are the receiver, try to have only one thing in mind: to let go and be willing to give yourself over to the strong emotions that may be surfacing during the massage. You will do yourself a great favor. Only if we are willing to give ourselves over to our partner are we able to enjoy. With this willingness, you are telling your partner that you trust his/her hands without reservation, and this is a precious gift to any intimate relationship. But you are also telling your partner that you have confidence in his/her ability to take away tension and make you feel good; in other words, that you have confidence that he/she knows how to please you.

If you are the giver, your mind should be on only one thing: How do I please my partner? Concentrate on your partner's body and on all the things he/she likes. The better you concentrate, the more readily you will "know" through your hands what makes your partner feel good and what doesn't. You will know where the flow of energy is interrupted, where the barriers are that your partner has not been able to talk about or wasn't even aware of—yet.

If you should find that your mind is beginning to wander, perhaps because so many unresolved issues from a day at work are lurking in your subconscious, bring yourself gently back by concentrating on your breathing. Intentional, even breathing will not only allow your body's energies to flow freely and fill you with warmth, but it will also quickly relieve you of tension and stress and let you focus on something more positive—the partner massage.

When you are about to begin a massage, be sure that you are not carrying any anger or rage within yourself. Even if you had no intention of doing so, you would undoubtedly transfer your negative emotion to your partner. Then your partner would probably become edgy, would possibly react with sadness or aggression, or might want to terminate the massage—without, maybe, even knowing why. So, be honest with yourself and your partner, and if you can't get rid of your anger, put off the massage to another time.

Besides inner harmony and composure, your hands are most important. They should be warm and soft, loose, without tension. But this is not always easy, since we tend to carry tension in our hands. So, it might be necessary for you to submerge your hands in warm water and follow up by gently rubbing a fragrant massage oil into the skin until they feel comfortably warm and silky smooth.

Try to follow the contours of your partner's body and to keep in contact with his/her skin. Think of your hands as a stream of water that is flowing around your partner's body, exploring and swirling about every hollow, edge, and valley. When you wonder, "How much pressure should I apply and how slow or quick should my movements be?", let yourself be guided by your own senses and intuition. When you think, "I can sense that this feels good to my partner, that he/she is enjoying this, that he/she got the 'message,'" acknowledge the validity of your own intuition. But nothing can be more convincing or gratifying than to hear your partner say, "Ah, that feels good."

Even if you have a "silent" partner, it won't take you long to learn what his/her likes and dislikes are. You will discover that you do not need to know a particular method or a special sequence in order to do partner massage; there are no tricks. You do not have to be a professional massage therapist. Sensitive hands, a little bit of leisure, the willingness to listen to your partner's needs and likes, and the willingness to allow emotions and reactions to surface—your own and your partner's—are the most important prerequisites to giving a loving massage.

However, should you be interested in some specifics, what follows is an overview of some of the most popular massage methods.

Massage Methods

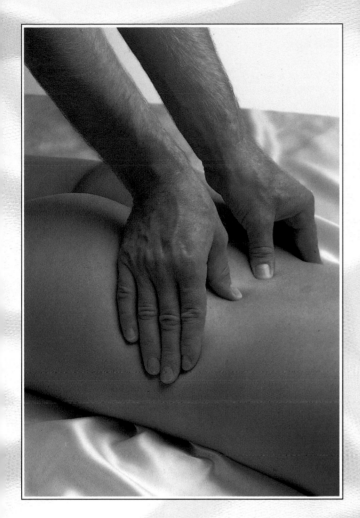

Classical Massage

Also called Swedish massage, classical massage is performed by trained therapeutic professionals; however, elements of it can be worked into partner massage. Classical massage requires knowing about a set of distinct kneading techniques and massage routines in order to achieve the best possible healing effect.

Stroking movements (*effleurage*), which increase circulation on the surface of the body, are used to prepare the body and skin for the treatment. The stroking is followed by kneading (*petrisage*), which will loosen and relax tense muscle sections. Next comes the spiral-like rubbing (*friktion*) with the thumb to detect and relax localized muscle spasms. Then there's the vibrating, or drumming (*tapotement*), of sections of the musculature, which is also beneficial for circulation.

Circulatory problems and chronic, often very painful muscle tensions respond positively to Swedish massage. As a way to relieve everyday tension, this treatment is an ideal choice; every trace of a hard day at work is magically wiped away. The pain of pulled muscles that tends to increase as the day wears on can be alleviated. Swedish massage is great for relieving stress and for giving your body new vitality. Since blood circulation is increased, you will only need to look in a mirror to see that your complexion is revitalized, which will add to your feeling of well-being. In this sense, Swedish massage is a beauty treatment as well.

In terms of integrating parts of Swedish massage into the partner massage routine, you can stroke your partner's entire body with firm and sure movements of the palm of your hand, and, if need be, relax hardened tissue and tense muscles with gentle kneading. While Swedish massage is routinely a method utilizing swift and energetic strokes, in partner massage care should be taken so that they are never too energetic. Your partner should never feel pain. If that should happen by mistake, be sure to lessen the pressure and go more gently.

Lymph-Drainage Massage

This massage method is used mostly for medical-therapeutic reasons, but it is also a preferred treatment in the cosmetic field. Fluids that have become stagnant in the lymphatic channels are freed by gentle, circular stroking of the tissue along particular points of the lymphatic system. This method is very effective for dealing with swelling of the area around the eyes and of the legs. Cellulite, of great concern to many women, is treated with lymphatic drainage massage. Migraine headaches and painful nerves often are the result of blocked lymphatic fluids and also react very favorably to this type of massage. Lymph-drainage massage is performed with extreme care and gentleness and is therefore a wonderful adjunct to a partner massage.

Lymph-drainage massage

Connective tissue massage

Connective Tissue Massage

With this massage method, you pull your fingertips along the channels of the connective tissue in order to loosen the parts that have become "glued" together and to make them pliable again. This massage affects different organs in the body that have become weakened or are hindered in their normal functions. Medical professionals have drawn up diagrams that show "tension zones" that are connected to specific organs in our system. The connective tissue massage is not quite as gentle as the lymph-drainage massage, and it is not unusual to feel some pain. But—and this is the positive side of it—the pain is a sure sign that the massage is "working" right where you need it and therefore will have a beneficial effect on the organ connected to the particular tissue.

Foot Reflexology

Similarly, with foot reflexology, when certain points on the soles of your feet are massaged, a healing reflex takes place in particular parts or organs of your system. The massage therapist Eunice D. Ingham developed this method, and was able to achieve true miracles with back and headache problems, as well as with listlessness and depression. The method rests on the belief that each organ in our body has a corresponding pressure point on the soles of the feet. If these pressure points are manipulated in certain ways, it will influence the flow of energy that is directly connected to the corresponding areas in the body. Foot reflexology can either revitalize these areas or gently guide them to relaxation.

Rolfing

Named after the well-known therapist Ida Rolf, rolfing is a method that employs deep massage to treat physical as well as psychological tension.

In rolfing, pressure is applied to muscles, connective tissue, tendons, and ligaments in a way that reaches deep into the musculature. This method is not always without pain. Rolfing touches both body and soul like no other type of massage. For instance, massaging a pulled or tense muscle may not only produce pain in that particular area but will often bring out emotional pain as well. It is possible to bring previously buried, traumatic childhood memories to consciousness—memories that have been repressed but have found their expression in visible, chronic muscle tension. Poor posture or chronic back problems often

Shiatsu Massage

This method comes from Japan. In shiatsu massage, the ball of the thumb is the primary "tool" since the pressure points (the *tsubos*) are often found in hollow areas of the body that conform to the size of the thumb. Shiatsu is based on the concept that the human body is equipped with energy channels, called the meridian. If there is a weak, or blocked, or too swiftly moving energy flow in this meridian, imbalance, pain, muscle tension, or loss of vitality can result. By utilizing specific shiatsu pressure, pushing, and pounding techniques, either along the meridian or

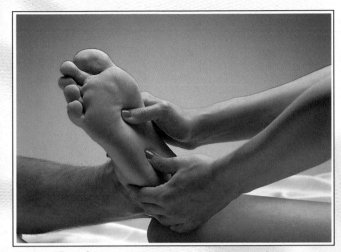

Foot reflexology

Rolfing

Shiatsu massage

are typical signs of an emotional burden that we are carrying around with us every day. It is possible through rolfing to bring these burdens to consciousness, to reexperience and then integrate them—a very worthwhile undertaking.

applied to specific pressure points, it is possible to bring the flow of energy back into balance. Pressure applied to the proper "vitality points" is said to remove the blockage of energy. This process isn't always without pain, but it's one that will lead to very positive results.

Partner Massage

The room is filled with gentle light; the music is playing softly; your hands, touching your partner's body, are warm, smooth, and filled with sensitivity. This is not a massage performed by a professional with years of experience. It is a special communication, without words, between two people. It has only one goal: to give your partner empathy and pleasure.

Massage is a language without words, an exchange of energies, that speaks to the senses. There is only one requirement: openness and receptivity to stroking and caressing.

Let your hands glide in rhythmical movements over the body of your partner. Envelop your partner in the finest scents that will provide a sense of well-being and allow for total relaxation.

Ironing out, pounding, smoothing out, brushing, kneading, rubbing, drumming, vibrating, finger-walking, stroking—everything is allowed in a sensual massage. However, only two people who want to impart to each other relaxation and pleasure, or who want to turn each other on, can make it happen.

Ironing out

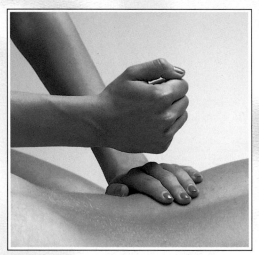

Pounding

Smoothing out

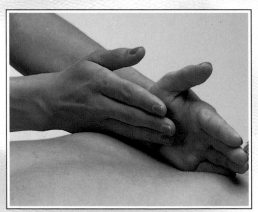

Brushing

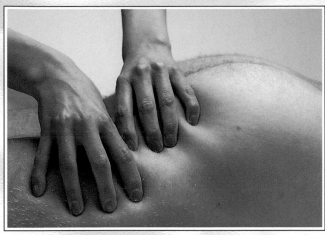

Kneading

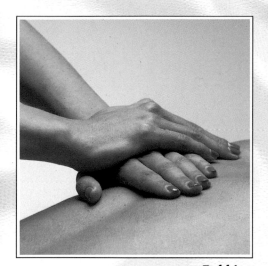

Rubbing

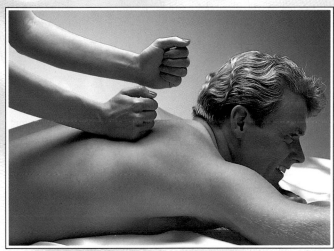

Drumming

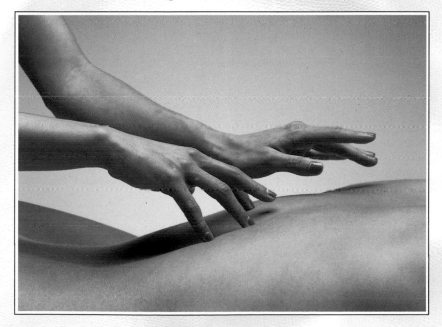

Finger-walking

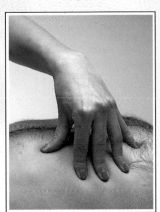

Vibrating

Awaken the Senses— the Adventure Is About To Begin

The Pleasure of
a Foot Massage

Western civilization does not neglect many parts of the body as much as the feet. Is it simply a matter of ignorance or are we ashamed of our feet? And it's our feet that must carry the heaviest burden all day long. Even if you are not overweight—let's even assume that you are at your optimal weight—your well-being "stands and falls" with the well-being of your feet. If they are tense and cramped, every step can be an ordeal. If they are squeezed into shoes that are too narrow, they practically scream to be freed. If the soles feel hot, they burn and ache. If the toes are pushed together, they are unsightly and pale. The pressure points between the toes are incredible. Our feet have only one wish: release, relaxation, and some tender loving care so that they can regain blood circulation. In other words: Our feet need lots of stroking.

Although partner massage has no hard and fast rules about how and where to begin, once it becomes clear how much our feet have to endure it makes sense to start there. The good feeling created from massaging the feet and the subsequent relaxation that begins to spread all over the body, filling your partner with warmth and joy, makes a foot massage the ideal prerequisite to a successful partner massage.

The condition of our feet mirrors our connection to reality. It also is an indication of how we deal with that reality. A keen observer will know about injuries we have suffered, what we are defending ourselves against, what it is that we do not want to come near us. Would you have guessed that our feet reflect our emotional state to this extent? Be gentle, therefore, when handling the feet of your partner. You know now that feet are particularly sensitive and much in need of relaxation. They do not consist merely of skin and bones; they have countless nerve endings with connections that spread throughout the body. Our feet are also the mirror of our body on a small scale. Each muscle, each lymph node, each organ has a direct connection to the feet. So, if you massage the feet of your partner, you are in a real sense massaging your partner's entire body.

If you are in any doubt whether both the feet and the body are profiting from all this stroking, observe your partner's facial expression. A foot massage is not only very relaxing, but it contributes to real beauty.

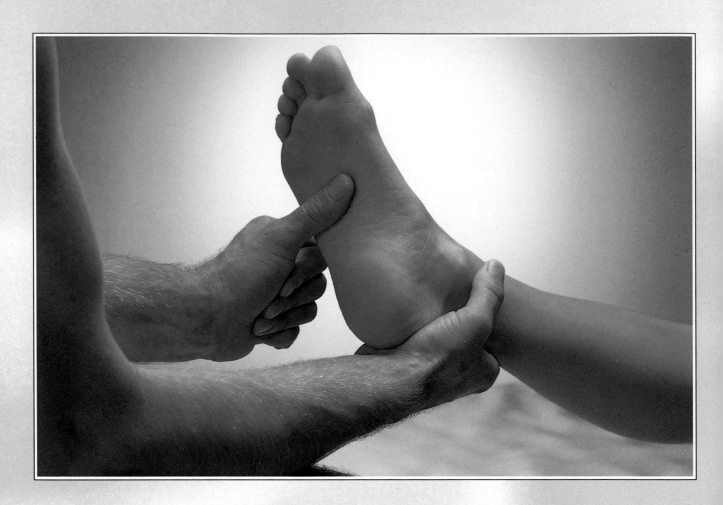

Hold your partner's foot in your left hand if you are left-handed or in your right hand if you are right-handed. Begin massaging the sole in small circles with your other hand. This can be done either with the palm of the hand or with your thumb (see above). Make sure that the pressure is not too intense since your partner might not be used to having his/her feet handled in this way. Your partner might even experience some discomfort or pain. Keep in mind all the many nerve endings that you are touching and stimulating. But don't be too timid; otherwise you will not be able to produce the proper effect, which is increased circulation, and with that increased warmth.

It is beneficial to take time for this part of the massage. It gives you and your partner a chance to make sure that you both feel relaxed and comfortable. If you do your massage on the floor, sit in front of your partner cross-legged and let your partner's foot rest on your legs. Or, you may prefer to use a thick pillow for this purpose so that the feet are directly in front of your hands. Don't skimp on massage cream or a gentle, aromatic body oil. If your fingers glide smoothly across your partner's feet, the enjoyment for both of you will be guaranteed. Proceed with a firm but gentle kneading motion until you can feel that the skin is comfortably warm (see photo on left). This is especially important for the ball and heel of the foot since it has to carry most of the burden. Now use

gentle stroking motions along the sole and top of the foot, from the heel to the tip of the toes and from the ankle to the toes (see photo above). This will loosen any last bit of tension.

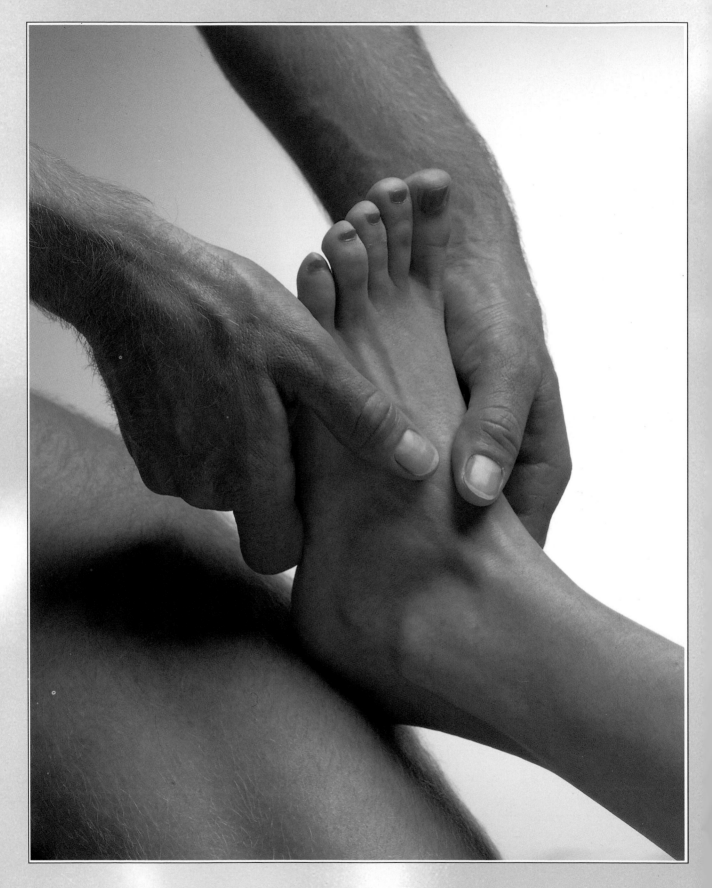

The next step is to stroke, knead, and press the upper part of the foot, beginning at the toes and moving towards the ankle and then back again (see photo on opposite page). Pay particular attention to the area around the ankle so that it will be loose and supple when you begin to bend and rotate the foot at this joint. With the tip of your thumb, follow the outline of the tendons that are running from the ankle down to each toe (see top photo). Gentle kneading at the base joint of each toe contributes

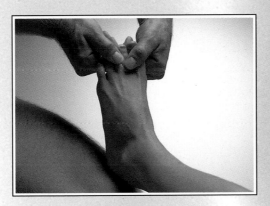

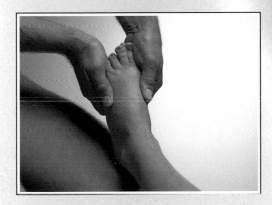

much to a feeling of well-being (see middle photo).

Now hold the foot in both hands, with the ball of your thumb on the top and your fingers meeting below on the sole of the foot. Systematically knead the entire foot and—without losing contact with the skin—pull both hands from the middle to the outside, as shown in the bottom photo. Whenever you change the position of your hands, do it gently and rhythmically—every part of the massage calls for your full attention.

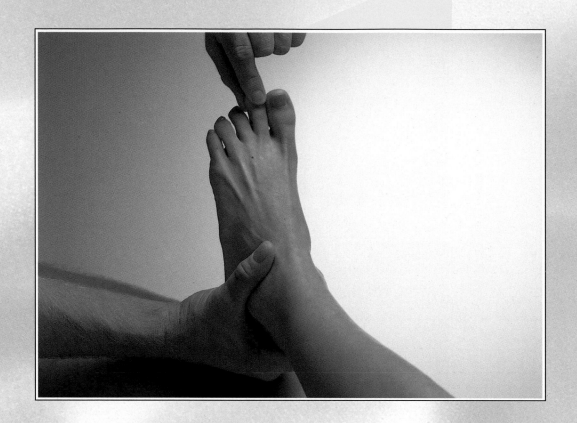

Now for the toes. Providing that your partner is not too ticklish, you can have a real field day of stroking and pulling that will make your partner grin with delight. First pull each individual toe gently away from the foot (see photo on opposite page); then follow this with a rotating movement. With the tips of two fingers, stroke both sides of each toe, and then bend the toes gently forward and backwards. Now grab all five toes in one hand and stretch them forward and backwards. Support the middle of the foot with the thumb of your other hand (see photos above).

The foot now is sufficiently supple and relaxed for the rotating movement. Hold the leg with one hand, just above the ankle, and make circular motions with the other hand holding the foot, as shown in this photo. Don't, of course, force the movement beyond what feels good and beyond what the ankle joint easily allows. If you detect any resistance or tension, you know you went too far. Make small circles to be sure that you don't overtax the tendons and ligaments.

As shown in the photo on the right, in partner massage the "work" on each part of the body ends in a quiet and loving exchange of energy. In this case, hold your partner's foot in both hands and share the flow of your energy with him/her. Allow some time for this exchange of energy to take place, and then repeat the whole sequence with the other foot.

A Total Feeling of Bliss:
Nimble, Agile Legs

In partner massage there are no rules and you don't need to do anything in a particular sequence. You and your partner decide the course of events. This book only offers suggestions on how you might want to proceed—without any restraints or inhibitions, cheerful, at one with yourself and with each other. You need to remember only one thing: to bring to this experience your imagination and your empathy.

After the wonderful attention you gave to your partner's feet, it seems to follow that the legs would be next. As with our feet, our legs carry a great burden during the course of a day.

Since your partner is resting on his/her back, it is easiest to start with the front of one leg. If you don't have a massage table and are working on the floor, it's best to kneel at your partner's side or next to his/her feet.

Let both hands glide upwards to the thigh, beginning at the ankle. Make sure that your hands are well oiled, particularly if your partner has a healthy growth of hair. At this point, it's all right to use a bit more pressure.

What is most important is for your movements to be flowing and rhythmical, which is easy enough to accomplish if you use your own weight. This means that you bend your upper body slightly over your partner's leg while massaging, shifting your weight forward as you move towards the hips and shifting your weight back again as you go down to the ankle. This method will make the massage less strenuous for you.

If you are using a massage table, just shift your weight from one leg to the other, according to the direction of your movements. The classic massage (or Swedish massage), which has as its goal an increase in blood circulation, involves reaching beyond the thigh, up to the hip, with stroking movements. Should you feel a little hesitant to do this, just stop—for now—at the

thigh. Using generous, strong strokes, move your hands on the inside of the leg, up to the groin, and then back down to the ankles. The down movement should be done with only very slight pressure since we want to help the blood flow towards the heart and also prevent it from becoming stagnant in the legs and feet. Try not to lose skin contact as you do these movements. Repeat the sweeping, stroking motions until both legs show good circulation. You might want to massage both legs simultaneously. If so, separate your hands at the base of the thighs and, going past the genitals, move up to the hip bone and back down again.

If, in the process, you should touch your partner's genitals, both of you should feel pleasure rather than thinking that maybe you went too far. If we did not have

these generations-old, alienating taboos about our bodies, we would not necessarily judge genital contact as being sexually motivated nor would we approach partner massage with concerns over what is proper or what might lead to a misunderstanding. Give these old taboos the boot, and, if you did not make a wide enough circle around your partner's genitals, ask your partner how he/she feels about it. If you don't feel like asking questions or if you don't want to interrupt the flow of the activity, "listen" for cues from your partner. Any discomfort will probably be visible. Should your partner say something like "Please, legs only," accept it without being defensive and allow the pleasure to continue. It adds vitality and fun to our lives.

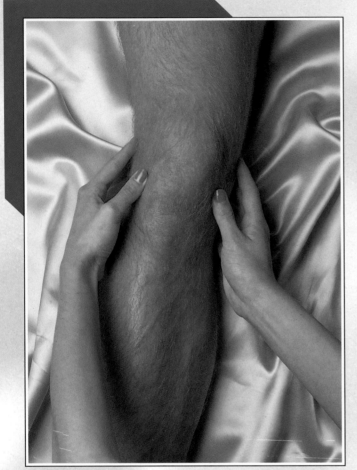
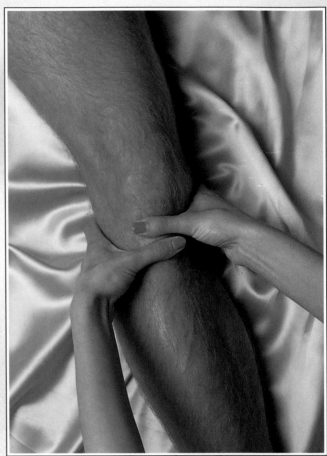

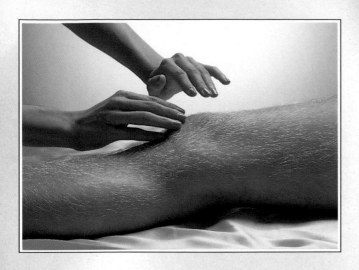

Pay special attention to your partner's knees because they are very sensitive, just like the inside of the thighs. Let the tips of your thumbs circle around the kneecap (see far left photo, opposite page), and gently press with your thumb into the indentations around it (see left photo, opposite page). Now, with all eight fingers, use a drumming motion—but gently, please—(see photo above), and conclude by stroking the knee tenderly in circular movements (see photo at right).

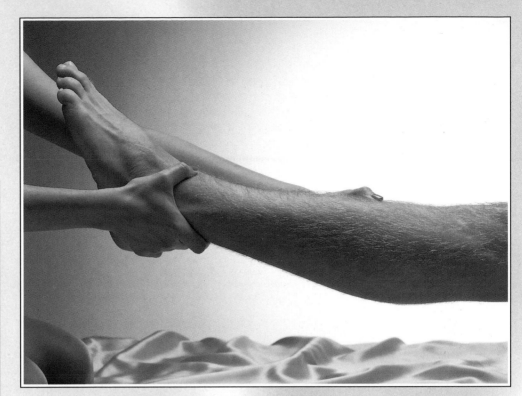

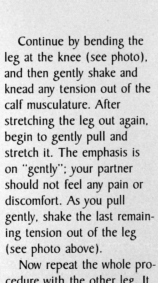

Continue by bending the leg at the knee (see photo), and then gently shake and knead any tension out of the calf musculature. After stretching the leg out again, begin to gently pull and stretch it. The emphasis is on "gently"; your partner should not feel any pain or discomfort. As you pull gently, shake the last remaining tension out of the leg (see photo above).

Now repeat the whole procedure with the other leg. It is also possible to massage both legs at the same time.

The next step is massaging the back side of the legs. Your partner will turn around on his/her stomach, and you will repeat the same motions you used on the front.

Some people prefer to massage the entire front of the body first and then massage the back. It doesn't matter which way you proceed as long as you keep in mind that the back of the knee is a particularly sensitive area—so be especially careful there.

Next comes the knee bend, which is not all that comfortable for some people. It all depends on how flexible and agile they are. Kneel in front of your partner's feet and hold the leg with both hands, as shown, and gently push it towards the hip and tummy. Push—gently—until you feel resistance. Depending on how supple the musculature and tendons are, this close bending back of the leg and knee can be very pleasant for your partner, but it might take some getting used to. So, start slowly and increase the bend a little each time you do a partner massage. Should your partner find it too uncomfortable, you might decide to skip this portion of the leg massage.

Remember that the leg massage, just like the foot massage, should be done with gentle, smooth stroking movements and should end with a moment of quiet holding (see photo, opposite page). This way, the energies generated can continue to flow, thereby increasing the feeling of unity you are sharing. Relax and enjoy your bliss.

Partner massage, this gentle antidote to emotional stress and tense muscles, is—and this might surprise you—particularly effective for the tummy region. For most people, there is no other part of the body that is so vulnerable and, at the same time, allows us to show our partner how much we are able to trust. This ability to trust is an indication of how good we feel about our body, which in turn is a barometer of our self-confidence in general. In other words, the extent to which your partner allows you to work on this area demonstrates how much he/she is able to relax and enjoy such intimate contact at the very core of the body. After all, the tummy is a vital center of the body that houses all the feelings that move in unison from the pelvis (our sensual and sexual center) upwards to our heart. That is why, once we get over any apprehensions, a tummy mas-sage can create such warmth and trust. For your partner to be able to allow you to take charge and thereby become defenseless in a way is an indication that a great deal of trust has already been estab-lished. It also calls for you to possess a great deal of em-pathy and gentleness. If you are too forceful in your movements, the massage will create discomfort rather than pleasure.

Begin by moving both hands, palms down, in circu-lar motions across the tummy. It will create warmth in seconds, spreading throughout the surrounding area. If you should be sitting down while doing the mas-sage, support your back with a thick pillow. This way, you will be able to relax. But it's preferable to kneel next to your partner—or, if your partner is on a massage ta-ble, to stand and bend over him/her. This allows your partner to see you and to watch the care you are dis-playing while attending to him/her. In partner massage, eye contact is very important.

You can add to your part-ner's comfort by supporting the legs with a pillow or a neck roll slipped under the knees. This allows the tummy musculature to be relaxed and the massage to be fully appreciated.

The circular motion should be done clockwise in the direction of the colon. Begin with small circles in the cen-ter at the navel, widening them gradually as you pro-ceed to the area under the rib cage and the lower pelvic area. If you like, you can put one hand on top of the other and thereby gently increase the pressure.

As before, when you de-tect a marked increase in body temperature, stop and linger for a while. Take your time so that you can both take in the pleasure you are giving each other.

A New Pleasure:
a Warm, Relaxed Tummy

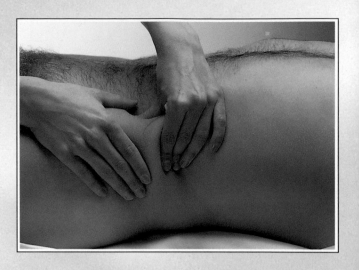

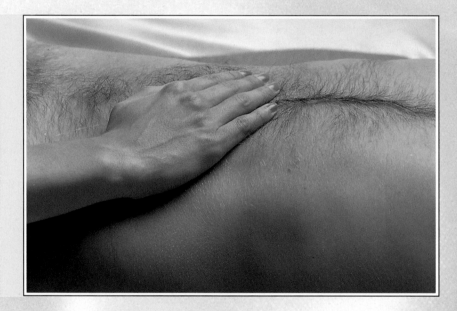

more than possibly tickling your partner. By the way, vigorous kneading is well tolerated by even the skinniest people.

Follow the kneading of the waist area with long stroking movements across the tummy—again, with the palm as well as the back of your hand. This will increase the pleasure. And remember to linger awhile with both hands resting gently on your partner's tummy (see photo on opposite page). It will deepen the trust between you as well as allow you both to fully savor the strong emotions often aroused by massaging this area.

As discussed earlier, emotions that have been aroused during a partner massage can be very turbulent. Most men have been taught to hold their emotions in, not to share their feelings, which makes them particularly vulnerable. This is new territory for them, so they sometimes show surprise and confusion.

Continue to massage the tummy diagonally from side to side, using both the palm and back of your hand (see top photo at right). Make sure that your hands are well lubricated so that you don't lose skin contact or interrupt the motion of your hands; you need to keep the flow of energy going.

The kneading of the waist area (see photo above) is very beneficial because the increase in circulation helps to flush out toxins from the body. Not to be overlooked is the cosmetic effect: The more you have your waist kneaded, the more your agility will increase and the size of your waist will decrease. At the waist it's best to apply a little more vigorous kneading than elsewhere; otherwise, instead of increasing circulation and lymphatic processes (see page 14: Lymph-Drainage Massage), you will achieve nothing

Take your time! This is really the most important thing to remember when it comes to partner massage. A perfectly executed massage method or any special tricks

are not what makes partner massage so exceptional; rather, it is your ability and willingness to get and stay in tune with your partner, to make time for him/her. By doing so, you are telling your partner: "You are important to me. I want to give you pleasure, to make you feel good."

To Breathe Freely Again!
Relaxing the Shoulders and the Chest

It's likely that the tummy massage brought out a whole array of emotions and feelings in your partner. Be prepared for something similar to happen when you begin to "work" on his/her shoulders and chest.

Behind the chest wall are life-sustaining organs, like the heart and lungs. This part of the body is often called the center of emotions and vitality. It is here that emotions gather and where they receive their vital energy. The more the body and soul are in harmony, the more relaxed and supple the chest and shoulders will be and the more we will be able to accept an exchange of warmth and tenderness with our partner. However, if emotions are constantly repressed, the diaphragm, the most important "breathing muscle," will be tense and breathing will be restricted. This does not only mean that we will be deprived of important physical vitality, but that our capacity to develop and feel beautiful and positive emotions will also be reduced to a minimum.

The emotions created through a chest massage are very similar for both men and women: sensual well-being and the wonderful feeling of being pampered. However, professional massage therapists, on the whole, avoid coming in contact with women's breasts. Perhaps they think that if you touch a woman's breasts, you will want to be sexual with her. Although this is not necessarily true, should sexual feelings well up inside of you if you touch your partner's breasts, accept these feelings—enjoy them—but don't let them interfere with the massage. There's no reason to deny either yourself or your partner this wonderful sensual pleasure. The breasts, with their tender tissue, react with a great deal of pleasure to the stimulation of a massage. Since blood circulation is increased, waves of warmth will extend all the way to the solar plexus and give birth to new and vital energy. An enhanced beauty of the breast is another dividend that goes without saying; it's a result that should serve as an additional impetus.

The shoulders are also very susceptible to tender loving care. Not only do we strain our shoulders by carrying heavy burdens, but so that we can handle the stress that bombards us every day, many of us, consciously or unconsciously, brace ourselves by tensing our shoulders. The result of this defensive posture is muscle spasms that create pain, often going from the shoulders to the neck and way down into the arms. Observe sometime how you carry your shoulders when you feel you have to contain such emotions as frustration, anger, or fear. When you are all bottled up, this rigid, tense posture not only gives you muscle spasms, but also blocks the flow of vital energies that your body needs, particularly at times of tension.

Therefore, make time for a good chest and shoulders massage as often as possible. Even if you don't have time for a full massage from head to toe, always include the chest and shoulders as well as the tummy and "work" them with tenderness and empathy. Take note of your partner's posture before and after this massage. The difference you will see will convince you of its value and will be proof of the miracle you've created simply with your hands and your emotional investment.

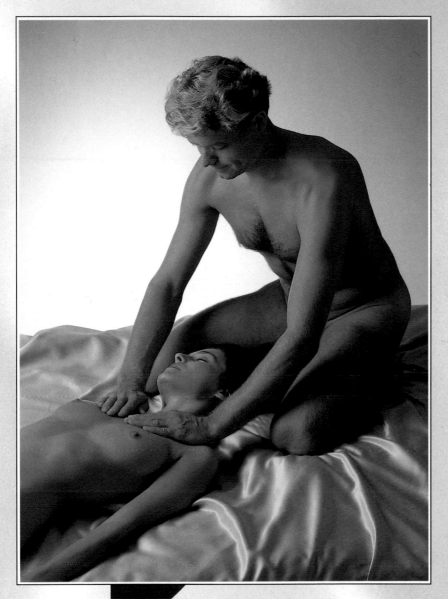

With the exception of taking a more careful approach when massaging the breast area of a woman, there is basically no difference from the way you approach this part of the body in a partner massage with a man. In massaging women, men should use all their sensitivity when their fingertips are touching the delicate tissue of the breasts. This tissue should never be pulled or unnecessarily stretched. You always begin by using stretched-out hands; then let the palms glide softly from the tummy up to the chest, between the nipples, and finally up the base of the neck. With these intensively performed massage movements, you will be able to create for your partner marvellous feelings of warmth and relaxation.

Now separate your hands at the collarbone area and move them over to the shoulder on each side (see photo on right). Then gently glide down on both sides until you reach the area just below the waist (see photo below). Without interruption, begin the upward motion, repeating the same procedure. If you do the massage on the floor, you might want to kneel behind your partner, with his/her head resting on your thighs or between your knees.

You can also kneel next to your partner. This position will be a little more strenuous, but you will be able to "read" your partner's face and see the pleasure that you are giving him/her, and, in this position, the two of you can have eye contact at any time.

Once you've generated enough warmth, let the tips of your outstretched fingers move across the whole area between the collarbone and the base of the breast. Use small circular movements and an ever so tender touch (see photo below). Then, slowly widen the circle of your movements to eventually include both shoulders.

The circular movements around the shoulders are of special importance. This is because the more warmth that is generated, the better the circulation will be, and the more relaxed your partner will be, and thus more capable of tolerating various kinds of kneading and stroking. Even if tension still exists in other parts of our musculature, if our shoulders have been thoroughly massaged we will be able to handle movements that would otherwise be somewhat uncomfortable.

Now move your stretched-out hands from the center of the chest in a sweeping motion up to the shoulders (see top photo, opposite page) and back again to the center of the chest (see photo above). This movement should be very even and rhythmical in order to achieve the optimum effect. Also, it's important to be tender and gentle as you let your hands follow the contours of your partner's body.

In the next massage mo-tion, move from the center across the breasts to the sides (see photo above). Don't spare the nipples, but just make sure that, if your partner is a woman, the pressure is especially gentle because the skin here is particularly sensitive. If your partner is a man, you might be able to apply more pressure since a male's musculature is much more compact and a more vigorous treatment is often appreciated.

A special treat for a
woman is a circular massage
in the shape of an eight
around the breasts. If you are
right-handed, begin with your

right hand outstretched at
the base of the left breast
and move it across and to
the top of the right breast.

The hand will glide down
to the side of the breast
again (see photo, opposite
page). At this point, you will
change hands without breaking the flow of a smooth and
gentle movement. Now move
your left hand with a gently
gliding motion underneath
the right breast and hold as
much of the breast as the
hollow of your hand will allow (see photo above).

Continue by moving your left
hand across both breasts up
to the upper area of the left
breast (see photo) until you
are again at the side of the
left breast.

At this point, the right hand will take over again. This "figure eight" movement ensures that the circulation will be increased to its optimum and that the skin tissue will be well stimulated. Both breasts will literally begin to flower.

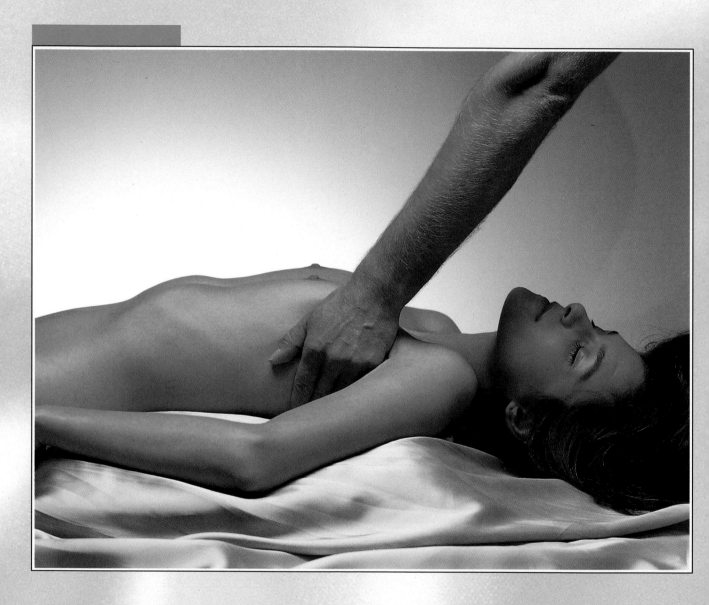

This blossoming is not
only a subjective feeling but
is also visually observable,
and it's possible to enhance
this state with the following
exercise, which, by the way,
is as pleasurable to a man as
it is to a woman.

With the palm of both hands, starting just below the armpit, move down to the waistline (see photo on opposite page) and reach with both hands around the waist (see photo below).

Now, while you move your hands back to the base of the armpit, try to gently lift the upper torso slightly off the surface (or as much as your strength allows) and hold it there for a few seconds. There simply is no other procedure in the massage repertoire that is more relaxing and gives more of a feeling of freedom and weightlessness than this one. Whenever there is a particularly stressful situation in your life or whenever your partner seems to have difficulty with deep breathing, you should give each other this gift of lifting and stretching.

To successfully conclude a chest and shoulders massage, use a wavelike "smoothing-out" motion from shoulder to shoulder. Try to picture the rippling surface of a body of water and let your hands imitate it. Move your hands from one shoulder across the neckline to the other shoulder. Spread your fingers slightly and keep them in very gentle contact with the skin as you stimulate the underlying tissue with a delicate back-and-forth rotating movement of your fingertips (see photo above). If your partner is moaning softly, it is only because he/she is experiencing so much pleasure. Your partner may be thinking, "When was the last time that I felt so relaxed and was able to breathe so freely, and could express how wonderful it felt?"

For a final conclusion, hold both shoulders, letting your hands rest gently as if to offer protection (see photo, opposite page). Linger for a moment. Let the energies flow, and try to make eye contact. The message will be received.

Arms That Can Embrace, Arms That Can Let Go

Our body tells the story of our life. It tells about our positive and negative experiences, our hopes, our fears, our unfulfilled dreams. It is a language that speaks louder than words. Our body shows what we feel—if we are defensive or if we are open. You might be surprised to know that in addition to how we hold our shoulders and our pelvis—in other words, how we walk, stand, and sit—how we hold our arms reveals a great deal about us. It says what kind of a mood we are in and how we view ourselves and other people. The way we hold our arms can either express "Don't come too close to me" or "I am eager to live life and to have new experiences." Keep these messages in mind when massaging your partner's arms. During the course of this massage, your partner may have some unexpected reactions that can be rather overwhelming. This especially holds true for men who still believe that they have to be strong and can't tolerate the idea that they may have weaknesses. Unexpected emotions for them can be surprising and often confusing. When this is the case, your partner needs, above all, your tender loving care and your acceptance.

Your partner should be resting on his/her back, and you should be kneeling next to him/her at about the level of the hips or waist. If there is quite a bit of hair on your partner's arms, make sure that you have enough oil or cream on your hands so that you are not hampered in your movements and sensitive hair is not pulled. Now lift your partner's arm up at the wrist with both hands, but only as far as necessary to be able to follow through with all movements. Make sure that your partner remains passive—that his/her arm stays completely limp. The movement should also be rather effortless for you as well.

Start massaging the arm with deliberate, long, stroking movements. Beginning at the wrist, let your outspread hand glide in gentle but firm strokes upwards to the shoulder. As you approach the upper-arm region, open and extend your hand even more so that you are covering as much skin as possible. (See photo on opposite page.) Here, as elsewhere, your upward strokes should be firm but gentle, whereas the downward strokes should be tender and light. The explanation for this is that, from a medical point of view, the goal of any massage is to increase blood circulation, which assists the body in transporting vital oxygen while speeding the elimination of accumulated toxins. These toxins are often a by-product of stress and frequently lead to muscle spasms. In addition, increased circulation supplies the heart muscle with oxygen much faster, thus aiding the pumping action of the muscle. Therefore, a massage employing these firm upward strokes eases the work load of the heart, since the venous system is located rather close to the skin surface.

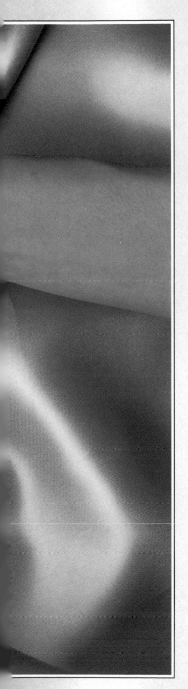

After several of these long up- and downward strokes, massage the inside of the wrist, which will add much to your partner's feeling of well-being. Turn the underarm and massage this area using gentle pressure with the tip of your thumb (see photo, opposite page). Small circular movements will produce literally showers of sensual pleasure. Alternate these circular motions with stroking movements upwards to the elbow joint (see top photo) and back down again to the outside of the wrist (see bottom photo). "Work" the entire arm in this manner. The results will be well worth your effort, and it's likely that your partner will tell you: "Ah, that feels so good!"

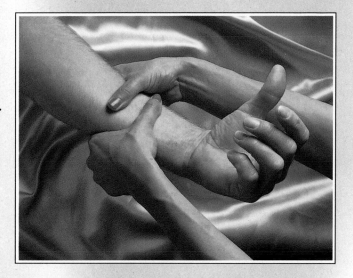

After this rather tender treatment, you must now become a little more forceful and vigorously knead the entire arm. This kneading of the long arm muscles is a favorite technique of women as well as men because the cosmetic effect is enormous. It stimulates muscle tone as well as tightens connective tissue, and will make your arms look gorgeous.

Proceed by kneading small areas at a time, from the wrist all the way up to the shoulder, on the inside as well as the outside of both arms (see photos). If you want to knead the arm using both hands at the same time, ask your partner to rest it on the massage table or floor and turn the arm as necessary. You may also, of course, support the arm as shown below and proceed with one hand. Find out which massage method works best for both of you, which creates the most pleasure.

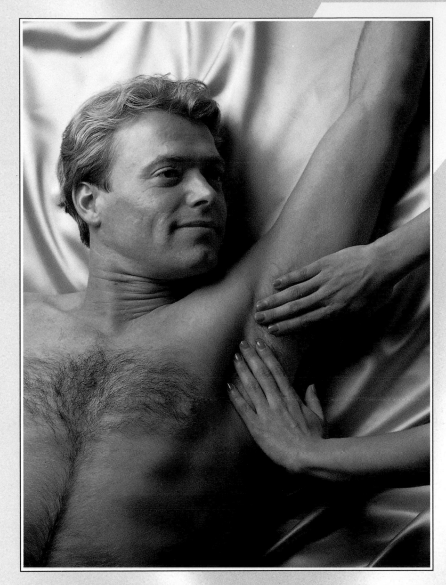

If you think you have enough strength, position your other hand at the hip, pushing downwards, while continuing to pull the arm upwards (see photo, opposite page). It will give your partner an increased sense of relaxation. This is particularly appreciated by men, who usually are not quite as agile in the waist and hip area as women. The only drawback is that it does require a certain amount of muscle strength on your part. It's best to kneel next to your partner at about chest height so that your arms have the best possible reach and you can achieve the greatest stretch.

If your partner is not too ticklish, a gentle pressure massage in the armpit area is very beneficial (see photo). It not only increases blood circulation but also increases the flow in the lymphatic system. Make sure that you use lots of oil if there is a healthy growth of hair.

In order to further increase circulation, while your partner's arm is still outstretched, vigorously rub the entire arm. Use both hands and move them in opposite directions; in other words, your left hand will be moving up to the shoulder while your lower hand will be moving down to the wrist. The result is a pleasurable tingling sensation, which is why this is sometimes called "fire massage."

For a calming conclusion, move your hands with tender sweeping motions up and down the entire length of the arm; then bring the arm to rest close to your partner's body. Proceed with the other arm.

Hands: Beautiful To Touch

Hands: tenderly touching and caressing, healing and helping, hardworking, cruel, even capable of killing! "These tools of tools," as the great philosopher Aristotle called them, give us the power to make our wishes and dreams come true. There is hardly a human ritual that does not involve the use of our hands: shaking hands when we greet somebody, holding hands with a loved one or a friend, exploring a body and its contours, expressing joy as well as sympathy, bringing messages or gifts. Hands—they have a language all their own! A gesture often says more than we want to admit. It may say that we are lonely, that we want somebody to keep a distance, or that we would like somebody to be close. Our hands will disclose how much self-confidence we have, how open we are, and with how much curiosity we approach the world.

Guidance for our hands comes from the "command headquarters" in the brain. Thousands of tactile nerves and many bones, muscles, and connecting ligaments give hands their sensitivity and dexterity, making them multitalented tools, which we use with such joy when we do partner massage.

As is true of our arms, our hands are not only useful appendages to our body, but they are the giver and receiver of the most sensitive messages and are always at our command.

Even though the skin on most hands is usually very dry, we need to use only a little oil for the massage. The musculature of our hands is constantly in motion, except when we are asleep, and is therefore very supple.

Stand or sit next to your partner, and let his/her hand and underarm rest comfortably next to the body. Take either the left or right hand—the sequence is not important—and begin by massaging the back of the hand, palm facing down (facing your hand). Gently follow the outline of the ligaments (see top photo). Picture the ligaments as peaks and the spaces in between as valleys. Let the tip of your thumb glide through the "valleys," one after the other (see photo below). The more gently you perform this motion, the more effective it will be. If this is your partner's first experience with partner massage, he/she will be astounded by the pleasure that can be produced by stroking the hands.

Gently press the skin between the fingers at the end of the "valleys" to stimulate lymphatic flow. According to reflexology, which insists that not only feet but also hands have reflexive connections to the organs in our body, these are special points where the flow of energy needed by the body can be positively influenced. By applying pressure, pressing the skin between two fingers for about a second (see photo above), blockages are removed and the flow of energy is reestablished. Renewed vitality now sweeps through the entire body.

Extra bliss is created by circling the tip of your thumb on the top of the hand. Start in the center with small, easy circles, increasing the pressure slightly as you widen them, moving all the way up past the wrist. You will be amazed at how the many small bones in the hand will react to such a subtle treatment.

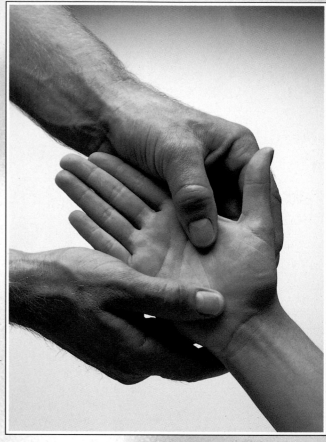

This is also the case when you rotate your partner's hand at the wrist while holding it with one hand above the wrist (see photo above). Rotate it five times to the right and five times to the left. This movement is particularly good for people who do a lot of writing, usually in a cramped position. Now turn your partner's hand over so that the palm is facing you. With the tip of your thumb, vigorously knead the palm down to the base of the fingers and up to the wrist (see photo at right).

Follow the kneading with circular motions of your thumb (see photo below), keeping in mind that the pressure applied should be less than that used at the back of the hand. Gently, let your fingers glide down to the tip of each individual finger of your partner's hand, starting at the base, as shown. It's best to do this movement with either the thumb and index finger or the thumb and middle finger, since both will allow you to gauge the gentleness and sensitivity of the pressure you want to apply.

All the movements that you have done so far will make the hand very responsive to being stretched and pulled both inward and outward (see photo). With this movement, you can exert a little more force without creating discomfort. This movement will also indirectly benefit the underarm. Depending on the work you do, this area is often filled with tension.

One of the most pleasant and tension-relieving massages is the kneading of each individual finger (see photo). You can begin with either the thumb or the little finger. As with all the other phases in partner massage, there are no hard and fast rules to follow. Both partners will discover what works best for them and brings the greatest pleasure.

The kneading massage of the fingers includes pressing, rubbing, pushing, and rotating each individual finger at its base joint. It is not very often that so much attention is lavished on our hands, but it's certainly well deserved. After all, our hands play such a central role in our life. Following a thorough hand massage, you will notice how grateful your partner will be.

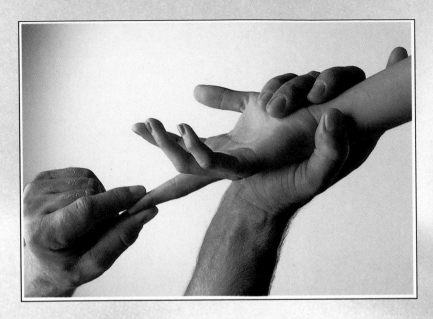

Finish this phase of the hand massage by pulling and stretching each finger (see photo above). Take each individual finger between your thumb and middle or index finger and pull gently. When you notice resistance, move your fingers gently back to the base of the finger. Make sure that the movements are soft and "flowing." When you are finished, let your warm hands rest on top of your partner's (see photo on right), and let your hands convey the tender emotion you are feeling.

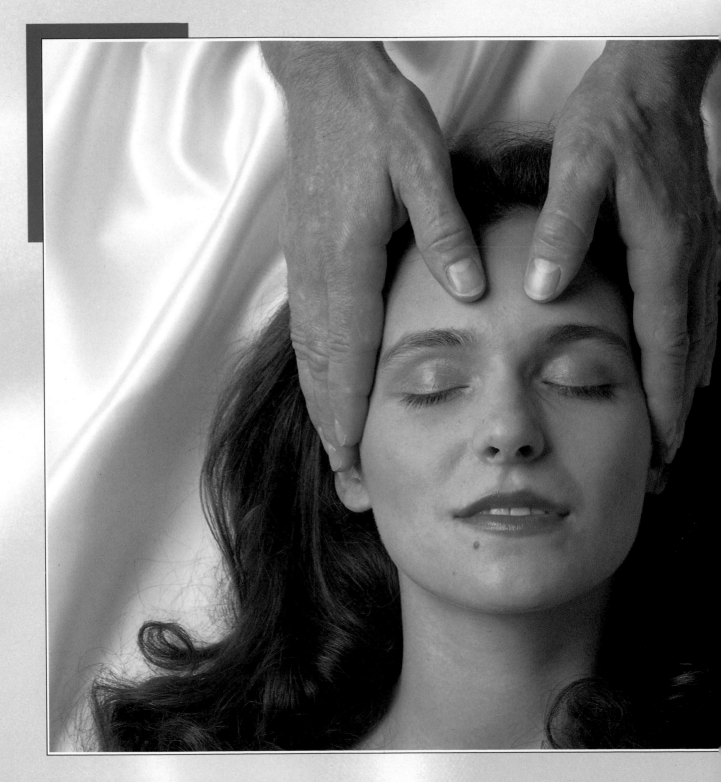

Magic Touches for the Face, Neck, and Scalp

In Western culture we are conditioned to live almost exclusively "in our head," which means that feelings are kept constantly under control. Instead of allowing our emotions to be felt in the center, which is the stomach area, they are immediately registered in the brain, and critically analyzed and judged. If it so happens that certain thoughts do not match a particular image that we have of ourselves or would like to present to the world, they will often be repressed. It goes without saying that this constant "head work" will not contribute to a relaxed face, neck, and scalp. If we constantly carry tension with us, our face will give it away. Only a relaxed face can mirror harmony and will radiate beauty.

The benefits of a facial and neck massage are twofold: It will make you wonderfully relaxed, and it has great cosmetic value, because the more relaxed you are, the more beautiful you will look. The feeling afterwards can be compared to the feeling you might have after a sauna or after sunbathing.

Maybe you are afraid that you might do something wrong since the face is such a delicate area. However, as with all other massage movements during a partner massage, if you concentrate on your partner's body, listen to the rhythm of the breath, and discover with your hands what brings the most pleasure and what brings discomfort, you will have nothing to worry about. Sensitivity is really all that is needed.

Start with the face. In terms of oil, what holds true for the hands is also very important for the face: Use only as much oil as is absolutely necessary for your fingers to glide easily across the skin. Don't forget to ask your partner if there's a special cream that he/she would like you to use. Although the aroma from the essential oils contained in massage oil are indeed nectar for the skin on the body, facial skin is much more sensitive, and allergic reactions are not uncommon. So, be sure to clear up this point before you begin. Also, any makeup should be gently removed with cotton soaked in a cleansing medium.

For the facial massage, you can sit next to your partner, or better yet, kneel behind him/her. However, some people find it best to sit on the floor against a wall with a thick pillow behind their back, and with their legs stretched out have their partner's head resting on their thighs.

The most beautiful way you can begin a facial massage is to let your fingertips gently explore the face of your partner (see photo opposite page). Glide along the

cheekbones; the temples, lips, nose, and forehead; the chin and ears. Feel the area around the eyes—here, of course, with special gentleness. Caress the entire face. Your fingertips will get to know every inch of this face. Afterwards, let your whole hand rest on the forehead (see photo).

Now start to massage the forehead with the tips of your thumbs, as shown below. First move your thumbs in small circles from the center

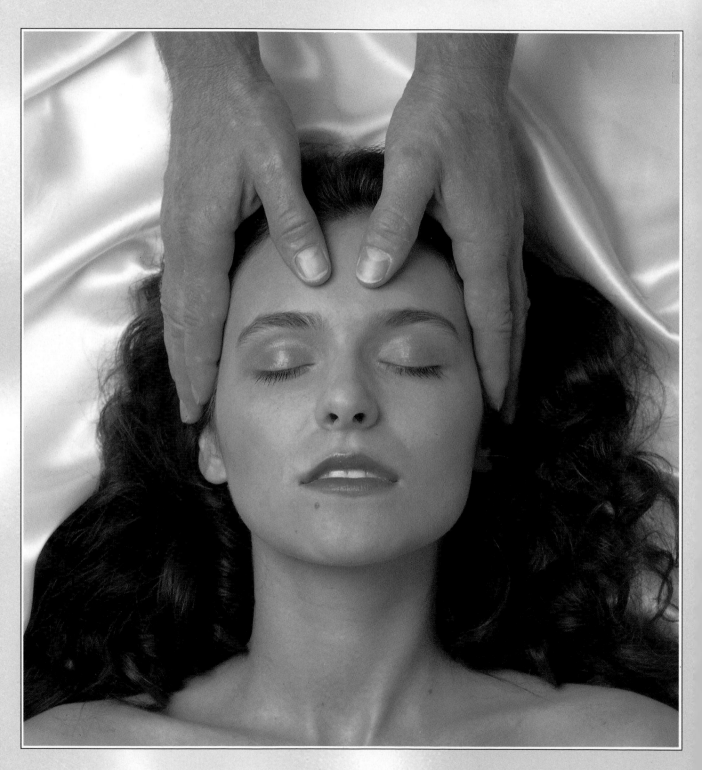

90

to the outside and from the bridge of the nose to the hairline. Next, move gently in a vertical motion across the forehead, beginning at the eyebrows and going up to the hairline and back down again (see photo).

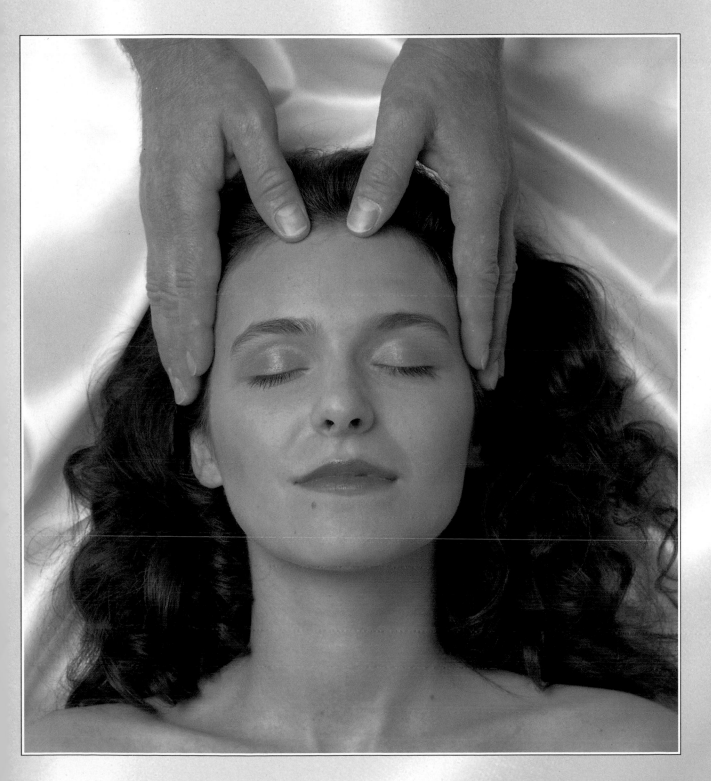

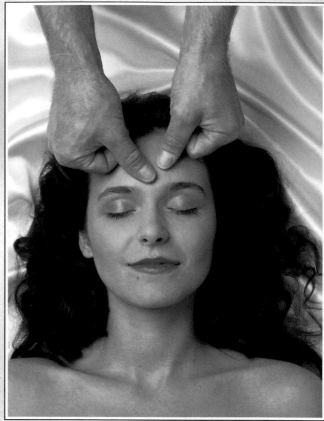

Now "smooth out" the forehead with diagonal movements. As shown in the photo on the left, use your thumb to stroke from the middle of the forehead to the hairline. This smoothing out of the furrows feels particularly good because it alleviates pressures and stress and softens the skin over the forehead. Give those vertical furrows between the eyes and at the bridge of the nose special attention (see photo). Even those of us with the most easygoing disposition often have tension in that area and appreciate the gentle stroking.

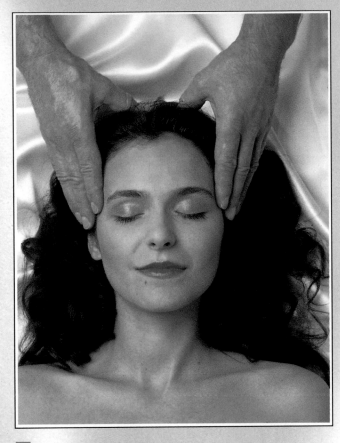

Complete this phase of the massage with the "forehead press" (see photo at left). Put one hand on your partner's forehead and reinforce this gentle pressure by placing the other hand diagonally across it. Afterwards, massage the temples and cheeks with small circles in a figure-eight motion (see photo above).

The next step in the massage is one that calls for the utmost in gentleness and sensitivity. Ask your partner to close his/her eyes and then ever so gently massage the thin skin of the eyelids and, in the process, the eye itself (see photo). Check with your partner as to how it feels and to make absolutely sure that you're not applying too much pressure.

Proceed now to the chin, under the chin, and the lower jaw, where you can use a little bit more pressure. With both hands simultaneously, move from the middle of the chin up and over the chin bone to the hairline (see photo at right). Men and women alike find this stroking very soothing and comforting, as they do the kneading of the ear lobes, which also creates a wonderful feeling of warmth. But be gentle; the ears are sensitive.

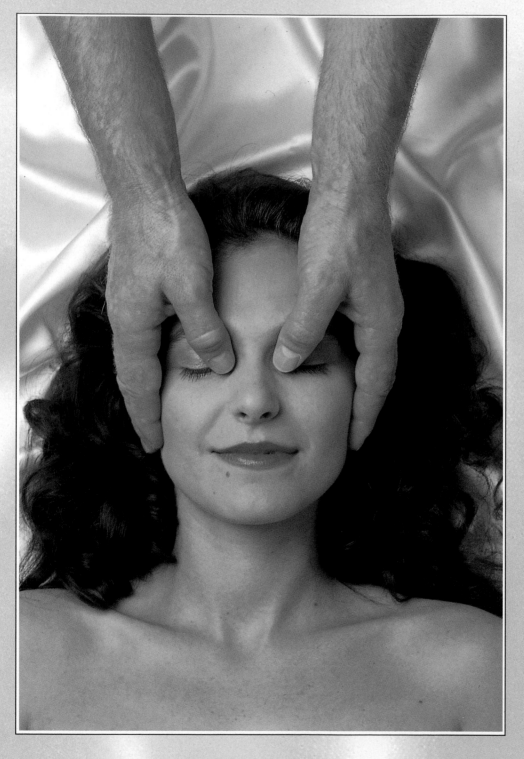

Now, move both hands to the outside of the neck and upwards to the hairline (see photo below). Turn your partner's head to the side and "smooth out" the area from about the middle of the neck up to the hairline (see photo, opposite page). You can do this with either the thumb or the entire hand.

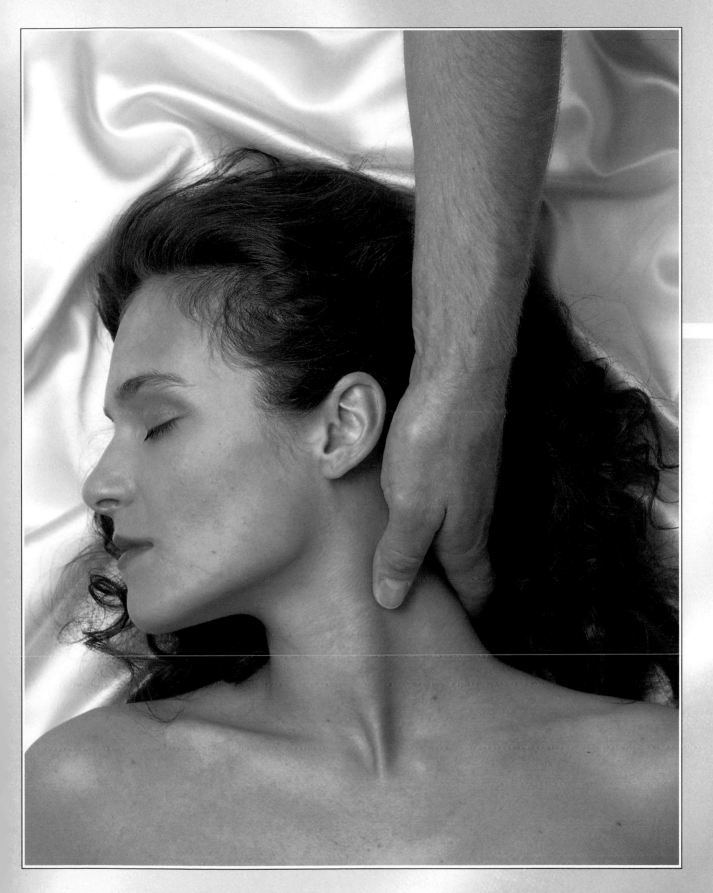

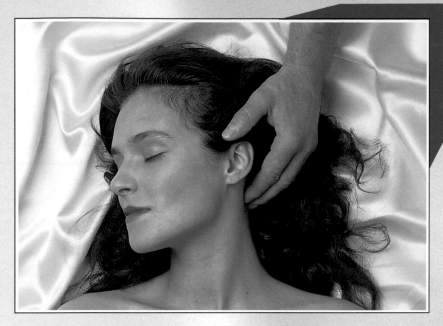

After this wonderful facial treatment, we proceed to loosening muscle tension at the back and neck area, where much of the stress of the day gets stuck. Position both hands behind the neck, with palms turned up. Cup your fingers slightly and move up and down the neck in a drumming motion, going down all the way to the spine (see photo at left). The next phase is a pressure massage in which you press down with your fingertips on the skin and remain there for a few seconds (see photo above).

This phase of the massage calls for extra sensitivity. Hold your partner by the neck and pull his/her head up towards you (see top photo). This movement is of particular value because it stretches the cervical vertebrae, which, in the course of a day, often become compressed and painful.

Remember that this action has nothing to do with muscle power; we are referring here to a gentle and tender pull, which is the hallmark of every partner massage.

All that remains now is massaging the scalp. Unless your partner has his/her heart set on the use of a particular oil, no oil is needed. Spread your fingers and move them over the scalp in circular motions, with a little pressure, as if you were shampooing. Do not lose contact with the skin, but make sure you don't pull on the roots of the hair (see bottom photo). Your partner will melt with pleasure.

Women who have made an extra effort in fixing their hair may prefer to skip this phase of the massage. Skipping it will not diminish their pleasure.

In conclusion, gently hold your partner's face (see photo on right). This will bring out in both of you an additional sense of security, warmth, and trust.

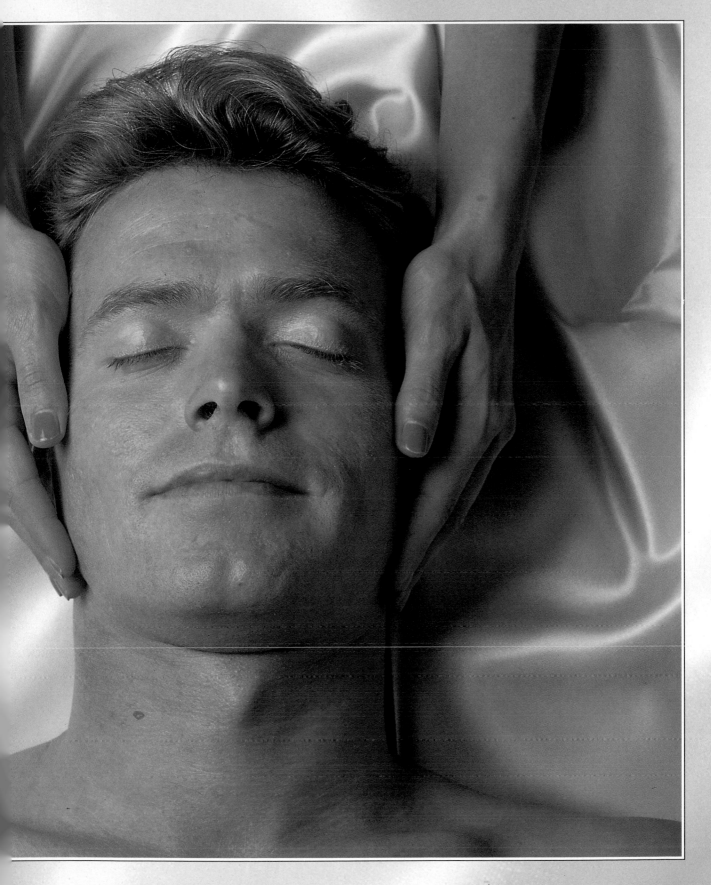

Massage for the Back and the Buttocks

"If your back is in good shape, so will be your physical and emotional well-being." These are the words of a professional massage therapist whom I met in Tibet, who said that he could "read" my back "like a diary." But after giving me a massage, he said, "Your back is supple, and you are in harmony with yourself, so you can be forgiving and generous. But your neck muscles! What happened? They are tense and hard, the complete opposite of your back. Let go—give in!"

At that time I had no problem letting go, but weeks later back home, when I found myself writing at my desk hour after hour, the tension and rigidity returned. Thank God that today there are professional massage therapists almost everywhere who can help us get back into the swing of things.

Our back and our spinal column are the center of our vitality. Emotional tension, stress of long duration, and physical overexertion are often the culprits when our back is in trouble. The state of our spinal column and the surrounding musculature give testimony about our emotional well-being and the fate of our individual organs. If you think about it, it makes sense to pay special attention to your partner's back and to give this phase of the partner massage its proper due, not only because the back happens to be the largest area of the body, but because it also plays such a central role in our life.

That the buttocks is included in this phase goes without saying. This is true not only for partner massage but also for most professional therapeutic massages. After all, it is in the buttocks area that we have a great deal of muscle mass and connective tissue, so we react particularly well to being massaged there. This is especially the case for those of us with sedentary jobs. Massaging the lumbar region and the coccyx proves to be very relaxing and will add a great deal to your partner's growing sense of well-being.

Your partner now is lying on his/her stomach. With well-oiled hands, begin with long, generous movements from the ankle on up. Reach with both hands around the calf and thigh (see photo on left) and move down again. The pressure that you exert is more intense going up than coming down.

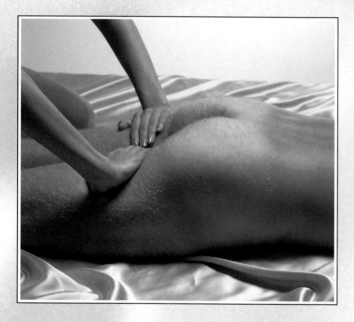

Now we proceed to the massage of the buttocks. If you are standing while doing the massage, position yourself next to your partner's buttocks (see photo on right). If you are massaging your partner on the floor, kneel either next to your partner or between his/her legs (see photo on opposite page).

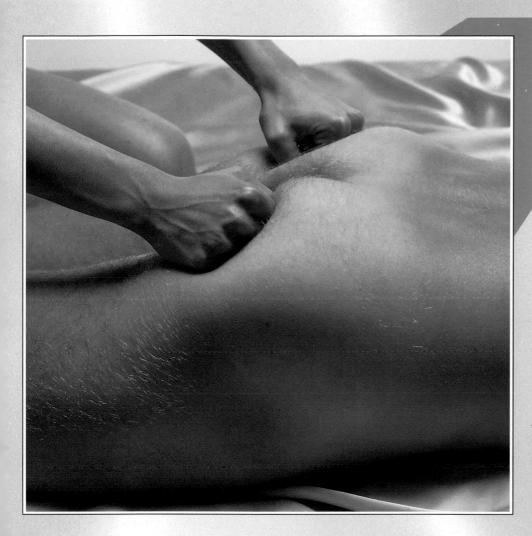

In massaging the buttocks, you can really put your energy to use. The musculature in this area reacts well to all kinds of pushing, kneading, and pounding. The more muscle volume, the more energy you can bring to bear. Make a fist and knead every inch of the muscles. If you twist your fists, turning them left and right with relaxed wrists, you will increase circulation even more.

Pounding the musculature with the back of your hands (see photo on right) adds still more to the overall positive effect, creating warmth, warmth, warmth all over.

Now put your hand flat on one side of the buttocks, and put your other hand on top (see photo below), and, in a circular motion, move up to the waist and down again to the top of the thighs. Just one word of caution: Be careful in the hip area. Many people are somewhat sensitive there.

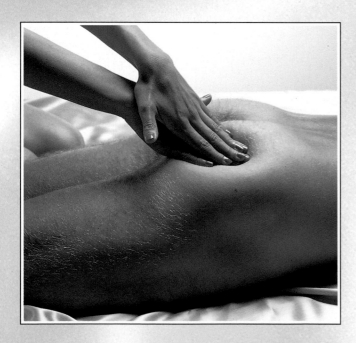

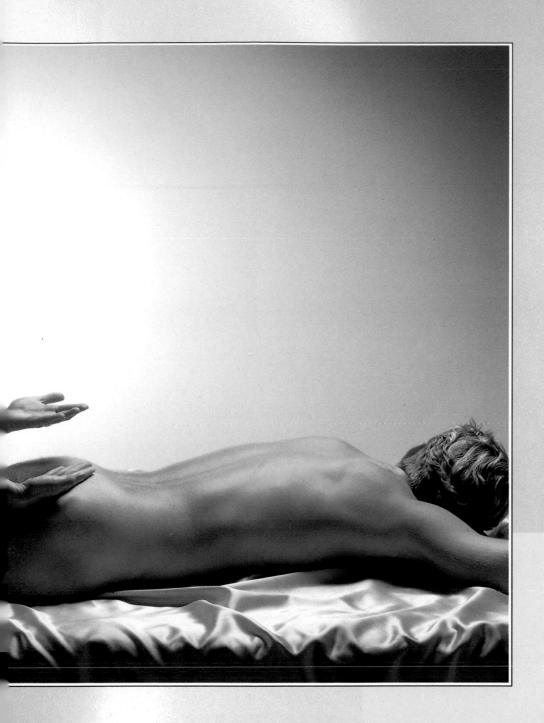

Before you get started on the waistline, smooth out both sides of the buttocks with your flat hands by moving them in opposite directions from the middle to the outside (see photo on left). This is an added stimulation for blood circulation.

For the massage of the waistline, use your entire outstretched hand and move in a slow, rhythmical motion from one side of the waistline to the other. Use the palm for one direction (see photo above) and the back of your hand when going in the opposite direction (see top photo, opposite page). If your partner is limber and not too ticklish, you might want to energetically knead the waist and hip area (see bottom photo, opposite page). Conclude by gently smoothing out this area with soft movements, starting in the middle and ending at the side.

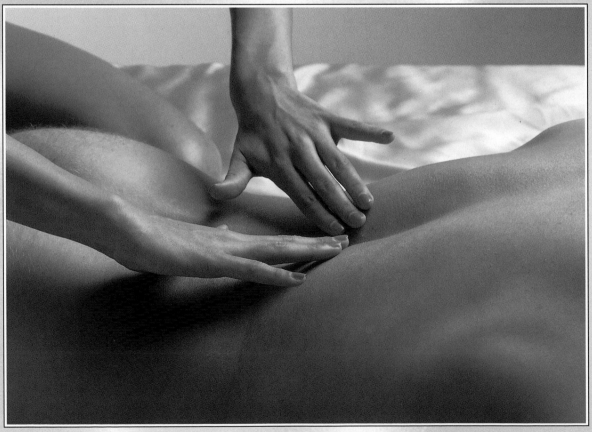

back (see top photo, opposite page). At the downward
movement, use only the tips
of your fingers and let them
gently glide along the hollow
of the back (see bottom
photo, opposite page).

Before you begin the back
massage, make sure that you
have enough massage oil on
hand. It's especially important for your hands to be
able to glide easily over the
skin. Your partner can
choose how to hold his/her
head: either on the arms
crossed in front, or to either
side of the body. You should
be leaning over your partner,
as shown in the top photo on
the opposite page, unless
you are standing up, in which
case you should be standing
next to him/her, as shown in
the photo on the right.

Use the palm of your
hands and with strong movements push your partner's
back "up," beginning at the
lumbar region and going all
the way to the cervical vertebrae, covering the entire

Now smooth out the entire length of the spine by putting one hand on top of the other and moving with gentle pressure from vertebra to vertebra, stimulating the adjacent area. On the way down from the neck to the lumbar region, let your outstretched hands glide along both sides of the spinal column, massaging the long muscles that give our posture support.

Now tilt your hands at the wrists and massage both shoulder blades, starting in the middle and moving in an arch to the outside of the shoulders.

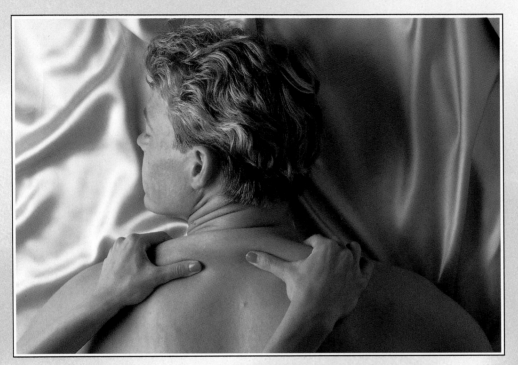

The next step is kneading the shoulders and the neck (see top photo). Although everybody benefits from this phase because it contributes so much to an overall feeling of relaxation, people who suffer pain from the so-called "shoulder-neck syndrome" will be especially grateful. With your hands either on top of each other on one shoulder blade (see bottom photo) or on each shoulder blade (see top photo, opposite page), move in circular motions over the area. Pay special attention to the musculature around the shoulder blade. And be careful if you have long fingernails.

The next phase calls for a great deal of sensitivity—as well as caution if you have long fingernails. "Walk" across the skin as if you were trailing your hands through sand on the beach. Start at the neck and shoulders and go all the way down to the buttocks. Putting it another way: Let your hands glide down the back with your fingers spread out slightly and your fingertips pushing into the skin. As you "walk" back up again, stay close to the spine and apply gentle pressure to each vertebra (see photo on right). Ask your partner to turn his/her head to the side to keep from getting a stiff neck.

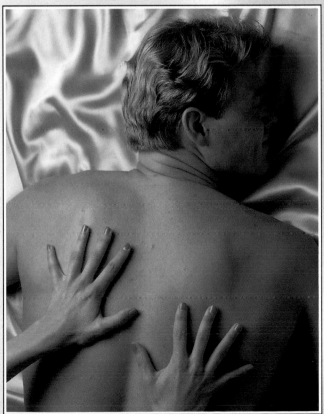

For the next step, it's best to change your position. If you are working with a massage table, stand behind your partner's head. If you are working on the floor or on a couch, kneel behind his/her head. This way you can muster much more energy. Grab the musculature that runs from the neck to the shoulders between your thumb and index finger, as shown in the top photo, kneading it to your heart's desire. One side at a time is the usual procedure. However, should you decide to knead both shoulders simultaneously (see bottom photo), you might want

to sit between your partner's legs again. Since the musculature in the neck and shoulders region is likely to be affected by stress and tension, it is often tender and sensitive; so ask your partner if or how many times you should repeat this particular massage motion. The longer your partner can tolerate the massage, the better he/she will feel afterwards.

In conclusion, "smooth out" the entire region of the neck, shoulders, and back. You do this by moving both hands in a sweeping gentle motion, starting at the neck and going all the way down to the buttocks (or as far down as your arms will reach) and then back up again. This will feel as wonderful to you as it will feel to your partner. Now let your warm hands rest a few seconds on your partner's back, as shown in the photo on the opposite page, and share the energies you have created.

A Massage Can Be the Prelude . . .

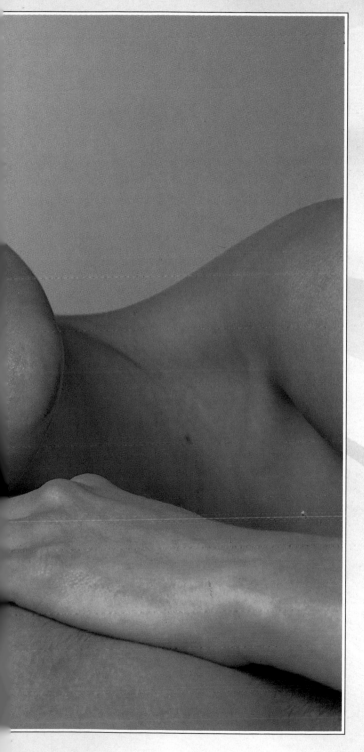

As you have probably noticed, the preceding pages have not been about rules and procedures that must be followed but rather about suggestions and tips. However, in partner massage, it is essential to be sensitive to how your partner is feeling, both emotionally and physically, at a given time and to acknowledge his/her strengths and weaknesses. It's very important to tune in to your partner with all your senses. Let your instincts be your guide. Let your partner know that you want him/her to relax, to feel good, and, if it feels right to both of you, to let the partner massage be the prelude to something more.

The goal of a loving and tender partner massage is first and foremost to wipe away all the tension, frustra-tion, and stress from your partner's body, face, and soul. But partner massage can also ignite the spark of vitality, making it possible to have fun, to relax, to enjoy life. And it can give you free-dom: the freedom to sense, to put an analytical mind to rest, and to allow yourself to listen to your body. But per-haps most important of all, partner massage can give you the freedom to shed old sex-ual taboos and role stereo-types. In this supportive and loving exchange, you both are free to let go of old hab-its of behaving and reacting to one another. Breaking down any rigidity that may have developed in your rela-tionship, partner massage gives you the freedom to talk to your partner about your own needs and wants, about where you especially like being touched and stroked, about what is fun for you and what feels good.

What better situation can there be for an uninhibited intimacy between you and your partner than this kind of exchange, in which both of you are more trusting and relaxed than at any other time and so completely tuned in to each other?

You have encouraged your partner to be free in expressing his/her feelings of pleasure during the course of the massage. So now your partner knows not to be embarrassed to voice sexual urges if or when they are surfacing.

At the beginning of this book, I make the point that men and women alike would give themselves up to loving caresses much more freely if they weren't afraid that, in return, they would be expected to perform. Unfortunately, many of us experience sexual performance pressure behind every touch or caress. And this pressure can make us avoid so many pleasures: the pleasures that come with skin contact, with tenderness, with closeness and warmth. Partner massage should never be a prelude to forced intercourse. But—and this is what makes it so wonderful—it *can* arouse sexual feelings that may naturally lead to sex.

When seduction is the main goal of a massage, in addition to your hands, bring your hair, lips, tongue—even a feather, or your whole body—into play. Your partner will be electrified if you follow the contours of his/her body with a light touch of your fingertips. Don't leave *anything* out, not the nipples nor the insides of the thighs. While you avoided touching the genitals before, they are certainly not off limits now. And if sexual arousal occurred by accident during the partner massage, now it is desired.

When your partner is drinking in, with every pore and every fibre of his/her being, every one of your touches and caresses, you will detect an ever so slight trembling and know that it is time to let your tongue glide gently over the skin. Alternate between slow, gentle movements and fast circles. To your own and your partner's surprise, you will both discover that your bodies have many more erogenous zones than you had suspected: inside the ear, the earlobe, the very tender skin of the neck (particularly at the hairline), the area surrounding the nipples (for men as well as women), the inside of the arms, the buttocks, in the back of the knees and at the back of the thighs, and the palms of the hands (particularly between the fingers). All of these areas will appreciate the erotic pleasures created by your tongue or a feather.

If you are a woman with long hair, your partner will love to be touched by it, and will even enjoy it if you swing it back and forth across his body. You can also brush the skin of your partner with your hot breath by moving your lips slightly above and across the skin. If you like, nibble on his/her toes. Remember, during a sensuous massage, nothing is forbidden, everything that you both like is allowed. Use your imagination and do what turns you on. Don't forget to shower your partner's body with a thousand little kisses, look deep into his/her eyes, and whisper exciting words in his/her ear.

To repeat: Touching the genitals during the partner massage was only inadvertent and not meant to excite, but when partner massage is a prelude to something more, you want to arouse your partner sexually. Maybe you even want to tease your partner a little, while he/she must hold still, waiting for the embrace so longed for.

We must remember that the genitals are not disconnected body parts but belong to the whole (physical and psychological) person. Of course, touching them will arouse pleasure, but much of the excitement is influenced by our imagination—in other words, comes from our head. This means—and it may come as a surprise to you—that the brain is the center of the erogenous zones. You and your partner alone decide, with the help of your instincts and your senses, how much you want to stimulate each other, how much you want to turn each other on.

However, should you only have a need for tenderness today, the "normal" partner massage will be all you need to be happy, and you may not even want to go further. When this is the case, just hold each other for a little while after this wonderful "journey across the body" before you face the world again.

Should you, on the other
hand, be in the mood for
sex, your bodies will be wonderfully relaxed and agile,
you will already share a very
special closeness, and you

will be ready to share yourselves completely. Enjoy!
    The time after having
shared a partner massage is
ideal for playing, for experi-
menting, for trying something
new and unusual—how won-
derful life can be!

Partner massage is one of the most wonderful ways of touching, fulfilling all your longings for warmth and love. Allow yourselves this extraordinary pleasure as much as possible, bask in it, let it carry you away. Let yourselves be gently relaxed or sexually aroused. Pamper yourselves; spoil your partner with imagination and devotion. And if you should find yourselves in the mood for more, be assured that partner massage is the best prelude to making love.